Entwined in Time

Linda Petroff

To Bob.
It's a blessing to be
entwined in time with you
Linda 2/20/23

Ten | 16
PRESS

www.ten16press.com - Waukesha, WI

Entwined in Time
Copyrighted © 2022 by Linda Petroff
ISBN 9781645384298
First Edition

Entwined in Time
by Linda Petroff
Photography courtesy of Alex Hui & Matt Warren

For information, please contact:

www.ten16press.com
Waukesha, WI

This book is dedicated to my daughters, Amanda and Nicole, who have contributed a wealth of experiences, insight and love to my life.
They are truly an inspiration and a blessing.

Table of Contents

THE HOUSE
ON THE CORNER

Finding a House

For seven years our search went on,
from one house to the next.
The asking price for shoddy work
left both of us perplexed.

One night we had gone out to eat
for a birthday family function,
unwittingly to destiny,
a place called Milton Junction.

At dinner's end we went to see
a house there, up for sale.
Pete heard of it just recently,
but we had no details.

Driving down the county road
the house came into sight.
Pete asked, "What do you think of it?"
I said, "What's not to like?"

After filling out some finance forms,
we were allowed a tour.
Dimly lit with low-watt bulbs,
things were a bit obscured.

But through it all, we still observed
the glory of the place.
The craftsmanship and detail
were displayed in every space.

The house was old, Victorian,
a spectacle to see,
a style that was well known and loved
at the turn of the century.

I thought of how it must have been
without electricity.
No power tools to serve their trade,
just skilled dexterity.

Rummage sale days were just the time
to meet the people there.
Happy, warm, and open,
the atmosphere was rare.

The grocery store and clinic
were only blocks away.
Just down the street was the hardware store,
that made it all OK.

After weeks of finance figuring,
we made our bid to buy.
Though we knew it needed lots of work,
we had the guts to try.

It took time to negotiate,
the price to strike a deal.
Then finally came the day we closed;
the fate of our future was sealed.

Peter loved to work on things,
to challenge mind and skill.
To have this project was for him,
a tribute to his will.

I love to rescue works of art,
restore them to their beauty.
To renovate this grand old place
became a sense of duty.

With the help of friends and family,
who selflessly volunteered,
we cleaned enough to move our stuff
and transported our furniture here.

And so began our adventure.
What lay ahead…the unknown,
when our family of four moved in
and made the old house our home.

December 30, 2021

The First Winter

Step one, we bought the grand old house,
family and friends helped move in,
but now to make it livable,
step two was where to begin.

Thick with nicotine residue,
as smokers had lived there for years,
scrubbed off the fugitive yellow-brown film,
beneath layers, true colors appeared.

Whatever solution had sealed the wood
was exceptional in its defense.
The finish had not been diminished at all;
to see the wood breathe was intense.

The hardwood casings of oak
stood proud and sturdy in place.
The tops, crowned in detailed dentil work,
to each opening, touches of grace.

The rich impervious grain,
the color of blushing-wood hue,
lend to each welcoming doorway
as vintage knobs usher you through.

Windows with prismed dimensions
now dance with the light, strong or dim,
compel you to look through the outside world,
while inviting rainbows to come in.

One window in particular,
not withstanding the heat of the sun,
had succumbed to its rays and was falling in,
none too soon, the rescue had begun.

In a bath of acid to ease the joints,
then a gradual increase of weight,
the Madison stained-glass window shop
then restored it back into place.

Encyclopedia pages
covered one parlor room wall,
the others, burlap and dictionary;
we had to remove it all.

Patched the cracks in the plaster,
primed and painted complete,
cleaned and resealed the floor;
now one room really looked neat.

Pete took the girls to school one day
only to find it was closed.
A snow day had been announced,
but we were not *in the know.*

Back at home he went to the parlor
to tune in to radio news.
To his dismay he saw water,
from the ceiling ran down to his shoes.

With bucket and plastic and hammer,
he quickly worked to contain,
gouging a hole in the plaster,
so the flow could then be restrained.

Oddly we counted our blessings.
What if our day went as planned?
He never would have discovered;
the mess would be way out of hand.

The roof had deteriorated
from the sap of the Walnut tree.
We had no choice about it now;
it sealed its own destiny.

So then we looked for a roofer,
but after the choice was made,
the work could not be started,
as the rain came down in cascades.

The weirdest winter ever,
it rained all season through.
Unlike the crooked man of prose,
a short-term patch made do.

Rudely awakened at 2:00 AM,
a ghastly way to begin,
from plaster crashing to the floor;
our ceiling had just fallen in!

Bolting up, we faced each other
and went to the attic to find
where the heck this leak could be;
one spot it must be behind.

A section was covered with wallboard,
revealing to our surprise,
the damage we found behind it;
the leakage had been disguised.

Each time it rained we worried
what damage we might find.
I used to enjoy a nice rain,
but now I had changed my mind.

When the roofer arrived, he was great!
Tore off the old roof complete,
put on new boards and sheeting,
and red Shangles, quite elite.

Of course nothing ever goes smoothly.
During his work he found
wood siding that rotted away;
Bondo had made it look sound.

Tore off all the rotted old wood
and also a north overhang.
Each was completely replaced,
structural soundness regained.

While the roofer worked his magic,
we had the chimney rebuilt.
Once held together by metal bands,
someday it surely would tilt.

To match the original mortar,
an identical color was used.
The cap was replicated,
the structural style was imbued.

With the chimney newly rebuilt
and roof and siding replaced,
we primed and painted bare wood;
restoration was fully embraced.

An intricate web of wires,
off the basement ceiling suspended,
from the day of knob and tube,
their use having since been amended.

It made us think of the changes,
since this old house was built,
when the dark was lit by burning gas,
to work and read and quilt.

This feature must be updated,
to a breaker box no less,
so we hired an electrician
to rewire the whole darn mess.

The original brass light fixtures,
with lion and bow shades invite,
to tell the story how Chambers
built with the knack of foresight.

Crafted in each ornate lamp,
through two different types of globes,
curved up, for gas then in use,
curved down, for soon coming light bulbs.

Yes he built with foresight and love
for his bride in the light of their marriage.
We hoped to bring it back to that place,
that our efforts would not be disparaged.

January 5, 2022

Lessons Lived

Then one room after another,
we eagerly worked to restore.
Inspired by each project's completion,
afraid of the rain no more.

The walls were stripped of paper,
paste was washed off too,
cracks in the plaster were patched,
primed and painted anew.

Every room needed more outlets,
as one just wasn't enough.
Pulling new wires from the basement
was frustrating, timely, and tough.

And each room had its own challenge.
We endured living through all the mess.
Solving problems at every stage,
for our marriage, truly a test.

One thing would lead to another.
Each project took longer than planned.
Nothing was square or even,
replacements no longer at hand.

Some days were worse than others,
and we'd question, *What have we done?*
Then something would ease our panic,
and we'd find the strength to push on.

The skills that had built this house
were no longer taught in the trades.
We learned how to do things ourselves.
Where there's a will, there's a way.

At the library doing our research,
reading books and magazines,
ignoring modern restructure advice,
to restore is harder than it seems.

We found a man of distinction
who knew plastering methods of old.
He worked with both talent and skill;
as a sideline, his time was like gold.

He did our curved dining room ceiling
with a finish to match the curved walls.
Pete fashioned a trowel for his use,
at the radius, toughest of all.

An idea I thought would be chic,
paint that ceiling "Stardust" like the song,
with special metallic paint,
to reflect in the light all night long.

I had access to Ralph Lauren brand,
to buy before market debut.
Though pricey, the color was perfect,
to apply it was all we need do!

Much easier said than done,
I cried after trying all day,
not brushing, not rolling, not coat after coat,
so we purchased a sprayer and sprayed.

Pete was at home in the hardware store,
back and forth several times in a day,
when he noticed he still had on slippers,
thought he just might be carried away!

We'll always remember that day
he worked on the toilet tank.
Immersing his hands in the water,
he'd forgotten the blue cleaning cake.

Frenzied with fixing the flow,
thinking better on later review
as he waited for it to wear off,
his hands, to his elbows, were blue.

It was truly a test of our "metal"
the challenge to work a new skill,
constantly changing plans to adjust,
overcoming our wearying will.

No matter just how precise we were,
computing costs projected,
after unexpected obstacles,
expenses were more than expected.

Time-consuming, the work lagged on;
we had our children to raise.
School, sports, and music, took precedence.
Gladly, childhood encompassed our days.

January 6, 2022

Exterior Summers

Though the inside was far from complete,
the outside needed work too.
Grossly overgrown bushes and weeds,
dead and scrub trees at each view.

The south and west slope surrounded,
with half dead hemlock and more.
We cleared the landscape of brush,
to see what the space had in store.

Pete in his engineer mode
decided to regrade the land,
on the south side nearest the house,
to improve the drainage, his plan.

The foot of the basement windows,
now covered by lawn, made it clear
that layers and layers of earth
had shifted there over the years.

He restructured the ground with skill.
When we dug up cement in our way,
found remains of a slate patio,
we imagined quite fine in its day.

With a hill only yards from the house,
preventative action was needed,
a retaining wall of stone,
for erosion to be impeded.

A serpentine contour design
to blend with the house's style,
Pete shoveled it all by hand,
and digging through clay took a while!

Then pallets of rock were delivered,
and with no expertise at all,
fitting each stone to another,
we started building a wall.

A weighty gigantic puzzle,
sorting depth and height the same,
fitting opposite ends to each other,
was a 3D, life-sized game.

We found new ways to communicate,
to explain how things should fit,
gesturing, to turn side to back,
or left to right, under, or flip!

Pleased with our work on completion,
we viewed the rest of the land,
and decided that we should continue.
Around each hill, a wall should stand.

More pallets of rock were ordered,
more digging to match the design.
Each summer another wall was built,
our landscaping vision refined.

Between two walls at the side yard,
massive rock stairs were placed.
With a bobcat, Pete and our neighbor
moved and muscled them into the space.

The setting now vividly guarded,
as the stone walls create a retreat,
you're free to walk up through the gardens,
safely grounded, your senses released.

I purchased a pair of old iron gates,
back at our previous home,
knowing we had no place for them,
but one day, their use would be shown.

Now at the top of our stone garden stairs,
they invite you through the entrance
and serve as proof to all who know,
time has no fixed frame of reference.

January 7, 2022

A Man-Lift for Painting

Though we had the house painted by others,
after years, needing now a new coat,
the thought of climbing ladders that high,
left us both with a lump in our throat.

We had rented a man-lift before,
and it made such a difference, we knew,
that to repaint this entire house,
merely using a ladder won't due.

After research and searching for years,
we answered an ad Pete had found,
though located three hours away,
our goal: to be safe off the ground.

It was old and not very well serviced;
the machine had seen better days.
When Peter went up in the bucket,
wires crossed, setting fluids ablaze.

For his poor widowed sister-in-law,
the seller was doing a favor,
but when the machine caught on fire,
to fix it would now cost him labor.

Settling for a sensible price,
to be free of his obligation,
we hooked up our project machine,
setting off for its new destination.

On the way home we discovered,
unbalanced, it swayed to and frow,
unable to go the speed limit,
taking back roads that we didn't know.

Though it took only three hours to get there,
it took us eight hours to get back.
The trip truly was an adventure,
navigation and braking, a knack.

Rewired, reworked, new batteries,
balanced, lights, and brakes,
bought trademark paint from the company;
it is worth all the effort it takes.

One side of the house every summer,
Pete sanded, scraped, and primed,
caulked and applied fresh paint,
colored details to accent design.

Touching up now and again,
repairing in nature's wake,
his paint job appears to be icing
on an ornate Victorian cake.

January 10, 2022

The Barn

The old barn predated the house;
it belonged with the previous home,
which now resides kitty-corner.
It was moved, as proof of love shown.

Chambers built this house on the land,
preserving his bride's family dwelling,
constructed as tribute of love for her,
her father's displeasure, dispelling.

Now the barn's roof was ragged and sagged,
with holes we had always seen.
We offered it to the Thresheree,
lack of manpower left them with no means.

In a permanent open position
stood two massive front barn doors,
supporting the weight of the structure,
binding pressure direct to dirt floors.

Some of the wood was rotting away,
some was clearly just missing.
The once sturdy beams were warped and bent;
through windows the weather came whistling.

In the back where there once was a horse,
"quite famous" said people recalling,
over the years a tree had grown
and kept one of the walls from falling.

Stairs to the upper barn level
were weakened and barely connected.
Water leaking in all these years
left them dreadfully neglected.

Only half of the barn's second level
maintained floorboards in their place.
What happened to the other side?
We could only imagine their fates.

The roof was the worst of all failings,
the shingles long since giving way,
exposing the life of the boards
to the predator waters, as prey.

Though we contacted people to fix it,
to give us a quote to restore,
barn experts claimed, after checking it out,
they could do nothing there anymore.

Pete, then convinced of its danger,
banned all from going inside.
Restricted too from parking our cars,
only stray cats snuck in to reside.

As for me, I knew it was sturdy,
even in its present condition.
"This old barn is not going to fall!
To take it down will be your mission."

It had served as wild entertainment,
held piñatas and a basketball net,
a chalk drawing of a dog on the door
would likely be seen there yet.

Its broad side presented a target.
In their playful and impish mode,
throwing rotten walnuts and apples,
our girls loved to see them explode.

It possessed a mysterious beauty,
not just for the use it had served,
but the truth that it held in construction,
its depth, too extensive for words.

Great beams endured ravaging storms,
each board held the weight of another,
filling-in for broken or rotted wood,
as if they protected each other.

Though they'd shifted on dirt floor footing,
it seemed only to maintain their strength,
adjusting to settle their load,
standing firm at each joint, to its length.

It had overcome decades of weather,
as exterior barn boards confirmed.
Noting loss of their paint and protection,
by the grit of their grain, it was earned.

But the city in all of their wisdom
decreed that the building must go,
unaware of our efforts to save it.
We felt that this was the last blow.

With the help of our daughters and friends,
we began the horrible chore,
to dismantle the structural artwork,
to grieve its demise evermore.

Trumpet vine had covered one side,
climbing over the roof, bloomed and grew.
To take it down, one more terrible thing
that this project forced us to do.

Then cautiously, relieving the boards
from their fateful exterior posts,
placing each one aside, at ease,
meant for salvage and saving, foremost.

Old metal hinges and hardware
rusted to reclaiming treasures,
various sizes of square-headed nails,
collected with gold mining measures.

An old metal barrel found tucked away,
still full with lumps of mined coal,
now abandoned, lacked expectation,
likely fireplace fuel was its goal.

We saved every door, beam, and board
with a neighbor's help to de-nail,
stacked it as neatly as possible,
our efforts to save it prevailed.

Then, to be witness to its collapse,
was the final step of our duty,
but true to my prior prediction,
it stood firm in its manifest beauty.

By all accounts it should fall right now;
it was up to us to convince it.
With the skid steer, lifted it side to side,
three feet off the ground; it shifted.

Then as we stood there watching;
waning painfully slowly, it caved.
Finally folding in on itself,
embracing the ground where it laid.

January 22, 2022

Living

When we first moved in, still adjusting,
as I walked up impressive oak stairs,
admiring the shape of the handrail,
something happened to me, unaware.

I looked down to take note of my hand,
now holding my pant leg aside,
lifting it off the step slightly,
like a full-length dress hindered my stride.

Bewildered and shocked by the motion,
I asked, *What are you doing, my hand?*
It seemed to have a mind of its own,
held my straight-legged jean, where I stand.

It was strange and so automatic,
though I'd never done that before.
It was a subconscious reaction,
as if channeling a long-ago norm.

What events must be swirling around me,
that time still recording, rewinds,
the blending of life experience,
present energy, with that left behind.

It won't ask you to remember,
but somehow you just can't forget,
the lives of people that you never knew,
and those who have not lived here yet.

Meals shared on cherished dish settings,
retrieved from the glassed built-in hutches,
a fireplace warming the living room,
flanked by griffins, flames fixed in their clutches.

Comings and goings on oak wooden floors,
with borders of inlaid design.
Did massive oak doors invite the world in,
or did they politely decline?

What music played, what company stayed,
all the laughter and surely some tears,
the love, the pain, and emotions strained,
all the living through all of the years.

The house just seems to invite you in,
to its natural sanctuary.
It's easy to find yourself inside,
where spirit and consciousness marry.

It's quite a different experience
to live in a very old place.
It has its past life and memories;
now it's your life, you feel it embrace.

After all of our work and endeavors,
there's a concept I had to adjust;
we say that we're living in this house,
but truly, it's living, with us.

January 25, 2022

Ghost

There in the window
or doorway at night,
a figure most haunting,
though not to cause fright.

Has tragedy left you undone?
Perhaps some act left unfinished,
or there in the moment of choice,
was your will to move on diminished?

Is your presence commanded?
A sentence deserved,
or guardian hallowed,
compelled to observe?

Have you knowledge divine,
transcendental existence,
or catalyst force,
answer prayers of insistence?

A desire to connect,
an occasion for query.
Concern for the soul
of a spirit most weary.

Compassion, anxiety, intrigue,
all possibilities heightened.
Glimpses intended? or chance.
When we face the unknown, we are frightened.

Are you here of contentment,
for this was once your home,
or do you remain,
as our fear...is your own?

March 15, 2003

Interior Views of The Chambers House

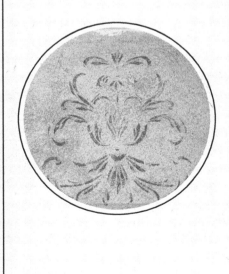

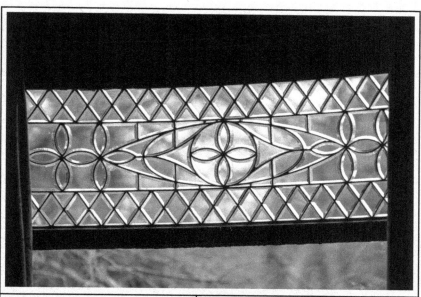

THE GROUNDS

Time of Renewal

Before the tender blooms appear,
before the trees turn green,
when the earth is in transition
as if waking from a dream.

The time of preparation,
renewal, and rebirth,
of raw anticipation
for life's merriment and mirth.

A season filled with ice and snow,
as far as the eye could see,
melts away in a few warm days,
and is all but a memory.

With winter's good-bye waves of frost,
his season is now past.
The earth awakens from repose;
we sow and plant at last.

February 18, 2012

Planning a Garden

I ardently anticipate
renewed ground,
thawed and black.

Anxiously do I await
the sun
to warm my back.

As I thoughtfully manipulate
the
catalysts within.

Attentively to stimulate
the cycle
to begin.

I dig and sift and cultivate,
life through
my fingers pass.

At the garden's edge deliberate,
poised
in dormant grass.

The earth and I to orchestrate,
a sensory
delight.

The landscape will proliferate,
a masterpiece
of life.

February 13, 2002

Lilacs

A year of waiting has ended,
and patience presents our reward.
All is the way it's intended;
the blossoms of spring are restored.

Early, most hardy and eager,
surviving uncertain spring nights,
their buds have no wish to beleaguer;
their timing, no matter, is right.

On the tips of extended limbs,
gently sway these tempting bouquets,
compelled by their offer, drawn in,
sweet as spun sugar their sprays.

They open, releasing a perfume,
the world has been waiting to breathe.
In that moment our senses resume,
our mind and spirit relieved.

A reeling intoxication,
induced with the richness of air,
creating such fleeting sensation,
replacing all consciousness there.

The cool heavy air of evening,
convinces their fragrance to linger.
The elusive scent, too soon leaving,
will return with the touch of God's finger.

April 24, 2012

First Blooms

And this
awakens my senses,
as though they had
been dreaming.

A moment
alive in remembrance,
of seasons that altered
life's meaning.

A breeze
draws my breath intermingling,
with earth's own passion
is teeming.

A color
embodies unquestioned,
even as time
is impeding.

Spring

The wind blows soft, thin covers off curled-up sleeping sprouts.
Buds peak through earthen curtains to see the sun come out.
Now finally the evergreens have company again,
and nature greets the spring like a loving, long-lost friend.

Breezes waft with fragrant blooms as if they were the fruit.
Bees and bugs and butterflies offer no dispute.
Sweet nectar keeps them busy; they gather while they may,
and liquid sap from broken limbs supplies a rich buffet.

Willows don their spring attire on graceful yellow whips
and make me feel nearby there rests a glass of mint julep.
The wind has found its equal in their consummate display;
each complements the other as they dance and bend and sway.

Trees stretch out their limbs to begin the season anew;
stages of their growth reveal fine greens of every hue.
Still, some decide to slumber, twisting to-and-fro.
The wind does not awaken them; it takes the sun's warm glow.

Spring's children cannot wait to bloom, no matter what the weather.
Near the feet of waking trees, daffodils play together.
High above in branches, the birds are busy there,
braiding twigs and stems in nests, the trees will proudly wear.

Yes, all of nature is aware, the trees, the bugs, the birds,
the wind makes the announcement in wisping, whirling words.
The sights, the sounds, and smells of spring, the grandeur of it all,
a spectacle of beauty, unequaled until fall.

March 25, 2012

The Nature of Things

I prefer to buy perennial plants;
it makes me feel as if there's a chance
for a minimum level of maintenance.

I read all the labels diligently,
but my efforts are thwarted eventually,
as my garden is changing continually.

Late spring frost, severe summer heat,
leaves on the menu for rabbits to eat,
drought and invasive weeds that compete.

Some plants need moving, three or four times,
for their optimal growth and their beauty to shine,
and sadly, some wither away in their prime.

The forces of change lie beyond my control.
I'll keep planting new plants, and nurture the old,
and take part as my garden's life unfolds.

July 22, 2013

Earthen Haven

Come, step into our garden,
you're always welcome here.
Free yourself from the worldly rush,
released from your cares and fear.

Mingle then with the flowers,
repose among the leaves,
live inside the fragrance,
and let your body breathe.

Have the trees watch over you,
pillars whose walls have no end.
Draw strength from their earthen systems,
to heaven, like angels extend.

Observe each limb swaying gently,
moving leaves, as if mobiles on threads,
each blossom is vital and lively,
and dance in our breeze as we tread.

Comprehend each diverse texture,
from petal to blade to limb,
revealing distinct variation,
concealing the network within.

Pattern, form, and structure,
the ultimate guide of design,
the fundamental arrangement,
in diversity, life is defined.

A true and authentic connection,
to persuade for a moment, to be.
Come center yourself in a garden,
and set your humanity free.

May 2018

Of Flowers and Weeds

While walking through the garden
I stopped to pull a weed
and couldn't help but wonder;
if I didn't intercede,
would they choke the flowers out?
Invasive is their greed.

The flowers need attention,
so I water, till, and toil.
Sweet blossoms grace the garden path,
the weeds, no doubt, would spoil.
They're tough and need no nurturing
to thrive in any soil.

Still in all my vigilance,
there's every shape and size,
some concealed suspiciously,
by look-alike disguise.
They seek to seize the fertile site
and fool the gardener's eyes.

But then I see to my delight,
a flower found its way.
The very means that brought the weeds
delivered a bouquet,
from someone else's garden,
a surprising new display.

A thought of life in likeness
and prudent now to know,
it is wise to sort the seeds
that our minds allow to grow,
by whatever means that brought it,
the intent, through words, will show.

Will you leave a path of blossoms
with those you see today,
or will you choke young flowers
with harsh words that seem to stay.
Will you try to fool the gardener,
or deliver sweet bouquets?

September 16, 2011

Garden Gates

Symmetrical bars adorned with grace;
curves forged in flame capture wind in its place.

Sentinels of sight, they anchor it all,
fixed and unchanging, winter through fall.

They keep nothing out. They keep nothing in,
facing each other the guardian twins.

Stop only our eyes to focus and rest.
A visual entrance, guide all who are guests.

A tempting allure, a true invitation.
Come see what's beyond, observe transformation.

Follow the path, leave nothing behind.
Bring all of your senses, and let them entwine.

Watching you wander, securing the space,
entice you to venture in the realm of the gates.

Though the plants are subjected to harsh, dormant seasons,
they return to this place without question or reason.

With wrought iron strength, through all they remain.
Steadfast they stand, in acceptance of change.

June 3, 2019

Autumn Trees

Shades that touch my emotion,
wrap me in mindful bliss.
In the depth of each color's devotion
lies the truth of the form that exists.

Beneath the breath of each hue,
enriched by its own design,
bring darker branches to view,
through contrast its structure defined.

The depth of its essence observed,
as if sketched by an artist's hand.
Awareness enthralled and allured,
as such complex splendor demands.

Each leaf owning blends of color,
from the outer to innermost branch,
in varying stages now covered,
the range of its nature enhanced.

Some vibrant and bright as if glowing,
others that burn unconsumed,
silent, and noble bestowing,
a glimpse of their grandeur festooned.

A few are gilded with gold,
still others of fine filigree,
as faceted jewels to behold,
or the work of skilled artistry.

Some feathery, weightless, and light,
or draped in regalia of lace.
Their branches appear to take flight,
and dance in the wind's fond embrace.

Many rustic as metal and muted,
as a crisp uniform they wear.
Their glory and wonder saluted,
by the evergreen's soldierly stare.

The oak stands robust and grand
in his seasonal armor, we view.
As his regal status commands,
his illustrious reign is well due.

The willow expresses the season
with ribbons of gold cascades,
never revealing the reason,
for her tender emoting charades.

Then there are those that impassion.
The basis of longing inspires
the richest and deepest reaction,
their velvet array stirs desire.

The sun in his sky can't resist,
reaching out to embrace their allure,
enchanted, compelled to assist,
their tribute and reverence assured.

Each morning they shall awake
to his gentle light's reflection.
The haze of the night they forsake,
and bask in his blush of affection.

Midday their colors are strong
in his full illumination,
no more shadows distorted and long,
only striking configurations.

Subdued, the evening sun glows,
through each filter his delicate rays,
sacred as stained-glass windows,
he honors their faithful displays.

Hills once fashioned in green,
mirror the sun's attention,
with kaleidoscopic scenes,
of color and light and dimension.

Unidentified shades,
exquisite in combination,
tone and luster invade,
to intensify transformation.

I watch the scene from a distance,
as it manifests hour by hour,
with the sun, share a lack of resistance,
my enchantment imbues them with power.

October 26, 2007

Snow Flakes

Each an individual,
the distant cosmic shrouds,
these fragile crystal waifs
born of winter clouds.

Drift now through the atmosphere,
silent, light, and free.
The unseen hand of nature
will guide your destiny.

To feel the hold of mother earth,
join your assemblage here,
unwitting force whose magnitude
affects each hemisphere.

At cycle's end and purpose served,
return to whence you came.
We'll call to mind your spirit
through the essence of…the rain.

November 2012

Wintering Trees

Symmetry of line,
enchanting to the eye,
nature's artful nudes
posed against the sky.

Unequalled shape and form,
in patterned limbs revealed,
perfection of design,
that summer guise concealed.

Storms of white occasion
to enfold their dormant grace.
Extended arms receive
an impetuous embrace.

In silken frost now veiled,
repose through winter's dance.
Prudently they wait
through predestined circumstance.

Prelude then to life,
as the season is undone.
Hopeful is the passion
in the spring kiss of the sun.

June 18, 2003

FOREVER YOUNG

Scissors Girl Solution

A terrible thing has happened,
an accident — the deed is done.
I'll hide it now from everyone.

I panic about it!

It's quite small in the scheme of things,
but I can only think of how
they may react to it right now.

Let's get past it!

Surely it will be OK,
better still, no one will know of this.
I'm thinking ignorance is bliss.

I'll undo it!

This stain will disappear for good;
no one will ever be aware.
When I'm done, there'll be nothing there.

I'll fix it!

I'll make them work — darn safety tips;
they're sharpest in the center.
All alone in my room, hope no one will enter.

I did it!

How handy are my pink scissors!
The antique rug looks better now,
not sure how that spilled anyhow.

The stain is out of it!

My seven-year-old mind at ease;
who sees that old rug anyway?
Relieved now, I can go and play.

That hole is just a part of it!

For my daughter, Nicole Petroff
(affectionately known as "Scissors Girl")

December 4, 2005

Tippy Chair

Gracefully she balances
as if she were on pointe,
instinctively adjusting,
the tension of each joint.

With small, deliberate motions,
her muscles now comply,
suspended between here and there,
gravity defied.

Mystic unheard music,
promotes this mental dance,
which occupies subconscious thought,
awareness to enhance.

A trick she knows and uses,
her classmates unaware,
the reason that she seeks out
and prefers…the tippy chair.

For my daughter, Amanda
August 10, 2005

The Boy on the Hill

It really was just a normal day
as I set about in my usual way,
but this one thing I now convey,
as a picture in my mind will stay.

I drove the city road until
turning onto the street of a sizable hill,
where a boy on a bike was enjoying the thrill
of momentum, pushing him faster still.

In his summer garb he was so carefree;
the school year had ended just recently.
Behind his seat tied creatively,
a fishing pole spoke of his destiny.

Then through his swift, unhindered descent,
with balance and skill and with full intent,
as if in slow motion, but not hesitant,
he let go of the bike in a wondrous event.

His hands in the breeze and eyes smiling bright,
his spirit was lifted in sheer delight,
a glimmer of magic, closest to flight.
I felt myself lucky to witness the sight.

A moment of truth he would now bestow,
like the boy on the bike on the hill below,
those moments in life, I hope I will know,
with balance and poise…to just let go!

August 10, 2011

Success

On my way to do some errands,
I saw two kids riding their bikes.
The boy was quite adept at it;
the girl seemed fresh off a trike.

The boy, concerned only with speed,
excelled past her; his taunting was clear.
But the girl was intent and deliberate,
slow and steady with purpose, not fear.

She was concentrated and bold,
preparing herself for the test.
Her new skill would surely prove to herself,
she'd surpassed her previous best.

Consistently peddling, focused ahead,
to the goal she was now fixed upon.
In a quick daring move, let the handlebars go,
clapped three times before gripping back on.

She had done it! and clearly was thrilled,
shown the joyful smile on her face,
and the visible burst of confidence;
a great milestone had just taken place.

The challenge was set by her spirit,
not competing, but personal skill.
The prize was her sense of accomplishment,
and the knowledge in power of will.

To challenge ourselves from time to time,
seems as natural as childhood play.
Gaining courage to act on your spirit within,
success is attained…day by day.

September 13, 2017

Childhood Pictures

The place, a moment in time,
a feeling strong and defined,
the memories set your mind reeling.

It was different when,
you were different then,
as your youth is so clearly revealing.

Now the sameness of you,
in your present-day view,
embraces the vision you see.

Who you were then,
revived in you again,
what is true now, was then meant to be.

April 20, 2021

Class Reunion

I would recognize you anywhere,
though the years attempt to disguise,
the child I knew when we were young,
in simpler days gone by.

From varied family circumstance
we assembled together anew.
The bell would ring, and we took our place,
and we did what we could do.

Teachers took on their arduous task,
impart science, math, music, and gym.
Some struggled and some learned easily;
all endured the changes within.

From counting and recess and coloring,
to growth spurts and braces and tests.
Through awkward and painful stages,
we survived it together, at best.

Then we all stepped out into the world,
when our classroom era was through.
Each of us went and took our place,
and we did what we could do.

In this moment, it doesn't matter much
what happened since then in our lives,
for we shared our youth, a season in time;
I can still see the child in your eyes.

March 27, 2017

Time in the Exhibit

My daughters and I went out to see
an exhibit, was that of Van Gogh.
The presentation, magnificent,
though only a part of the show.

The people who attended
provided an extra attraction,
I observed them in the displays,
taking note of assorted reactions.

The first section was a collection
of letters and notes back and forth,
from the artist and his brother,
to encourage, and chart his course.

All who attended stopped to read,
the arrangement was expertly done.
Up and down a path of frames,
from the ceiling, selections were hung.

As I was trying to concentrate,
this sound kept on tipping my ear,
a rhythmic and constant ticking noise,
made me pause to locate what I hear.

A women of substantial age,
entranced, enjoyed the displays,
strolling slowly and deliberately,
with a walker used as her aid.

Though she didn't seem to notice it,
or perhaps it was lost to her hearing,
came the resonating, echoing tick,
from her walker wheels and their gearing.

Through the hall of pensive readers,
who stood in mingling groups,
gently she strolled a consistent pace,
with a tick, her wheels lead in small loops.

Oblivious to those around her,
the world was her own as she knew it.
Standing tall as her stature allowed,
she'd persisted in life and went through it.

I admired her perseverance,
from a distance, affirming her grace,
in wonderment of her experience,
until someone intruded the space.

Self-engrossed, a girl hustled past her.
Neither acknowledged the other.
The starkness of their differences,
was clear for the eye to discover.

The women treaded intently,
walker ticking, advancing before,
in concert, her shoes ushered her forth,
they embraced and cushioned the floor.

She was prudently dressed for the weather,
in her cozy scarf and coat,
not willing to sacrifice her health,
but still came to the show, I must note.

The girl was dressed to impress,
and scantily clad to entice,
not exactly the clothes meant for winter,
but her choice never made her think twice.

Uncomfortably high, were the heels of her shoes,
which were surely not meant for the snow,
walking quick-step and keeping her balance,
as if she had places to go.

Her heels struck the floor with each strut,
with a cadenced clack, in her wake,
as they syncopate with the walker's tick,
their metrical blend, no mistake.

They never took note of each other,
though it seemed they had nothing to share,
the invisible thread of time through life,
in their physical rhythm, was there.

They clocked the timing of lifestyle,
locked in their personal pace,
with each tick of the wheel and clack of the heel,
Vincent brought them both here, to this place.

Van Gogh was obsessed with life's rhythms,
passion's thickness he pressed in his paint,
wild brush strokes thrust his visions through time,
bold and brash without pause or restraint.

Moment by moment he captured it all,
each portrait an insight sublime.
Inspired by his soul, his art made them whole,
pain and beauty innately combined.

The room was alive with the artist,
each painting displayed now surrounded,
through all of us spread, that invisible thread,
as the pulse of his presence resounded.

My attention then drawn to my daughters,
as his artwork enveloped the space,
all the faces and far-away places,
with his flowers, their essence relate.

As I watched them in the exhibit,
these moments intrinsically sweet,
entwined beyond time, by a pulse redefined,
somewhere in the hush...between beats.

I stood with them in shared awareness,
their life beauty and grace both, complete,
in our silence there, a connection so rare,
even Vincent's art, could not compete.

April 3, 2022

Angel for a Day

One Fourth of July weekend
as we sat in our living room,
Peter read in the paper
of a carnival starting soon.

Now, I'm not one for carnivals,
I don't enjoy the rides,
there are usually too many people,
I end up with a headache besides.

But for some strange unknown reason,
when he asked if I wanted to go,
I agreed without hesitation,
then thought, *What? I didn't say no?*

In moments we were out the door,
no discussion or delay.
Put on our shoes and grabbed my purse,
and we were on our way.

In fifteen minutes, we were there
and found a place to park.
Commenting on how close we were,
to find this spot, a lark!

Near to us there was a van,
with a couple in dispute.
Outside the wife "declared" to the man,
that spot would better suit!

With frenzied words hurled back and forth,
neither would understand,
that their child had gotten out
and now stood behind their van.

As the driver shifted to reverse,
Pete leapt into the fray
while shouting to alert them,
swept the child up, out of harm's way.

It all happened in just moments,
but lives on in consciousness.
We are all somebody's *Angel*
in their time of helplessness.

August 22, 2014

Salvation

When I was a very small child
each Christmas morning I'd see,
standing in our living room
the most wondrous Christmas tree.

Beautifully balanced splendor,
perfectly shaped and trimmed.
When I grew older, I realized
what a labor of love they had been.

More necessity than tradition,
a great savings in times that were lean,
but buying a tree on Christmas Eve,
meant the choices were less than pristine.

I saw the tree — bent, sparse, with gaps
and watched as my mother achieved
what seemed to be a miracle,
one you must see to believe.

She creatively wound the lighting,
colored garland strategically draped,
each ornament was so exactly placed,
to reflect, create balance, and shape.

Glistening tinsel, fragile and fine,
she thinly arranged one by one,
the entire transformation crowned
with a star; her endeavor was done.

Like that meager, distorted Christmas tree
we can all be balanced and whole,
circumstances that once shaped our lives,
defined, addressed, and consoled.

We can wrap our fears in the light of God's Son,
drape our pain with His mercy and grace,
ornament our lives to reflect His love
in our soul's most bleak, empty space.

Acknowledge our blessings one by one
to replace want and lack perceived.
Open our minds to follow the King,
through His miracle, salvation is achieved.

November 27, 2015

My New Year's Resolution

If you've ever watched a child
in their effort to progress,
you must admire their vigor
and composed tenaciousness.

Intuitive, a baby knows
to turn and then to roll,
to coordinate unquestioning,
their physical control.

To crawl and then to stand,
grasping weight against a prop,
they never seem discouraged
when unsteadily, they drop.

Eager still, they'll try again
with strength of will unbroken,
the force of nature whispers
sweet encouragement unspoken.

The very smallest item
gives a reason to explore,
to research the finest feature
of the dust speck on the floor.

Every waking moment
they take opportunity
to achieve a new perspective,
of the world they touch and see.

No preconceived ideas,
no judgment in their mind,
just the open arms of love,
faith, hope, and trust combined.

My New Year's resolution
is to live and love and grow,
to move forward, gently forward,
and be childlike as I go.

December 22, 2011

MUSINGS

Writing a Poem

I sat down to write a poem,
and this is what I found.
All of the words in our language
came in and gathered around.

Though the room was really quite small,
somehow, they all seemed to fit,
while making themselves comfortable,
knowing this was their chance to be "it."

There were positive words embraced by all,
sarcastic ones snidely poked fun.
There were bitter words that when spoken
make you wish you had bitten your tongue.

Words used for fear, hate, and anger,
reflecting the turmoil of life.
In a group they all mingle together
and commiserate in pure delight.

Words of sadness and grief are profound,
and the others, honor them here.
Respectful of their intensity,
empathetic support is clear.

Spiritual words that touch them all,
with healing words form an alliance.
Mixing with curative, medical words,
they converse with research and science.

Neutral words sit in the middle,
poignant ones rendering statements,
quiet ones calming the other words down,
and bold ones fighting for placement.

The smallest words are most confident,
knowing they will always be used.
The large words are like divas,
feeling misunderstood and abused.

Expressive and descriptive words
have enthusiastic presence.
Other words vie for their company,
to enhance their meaning and essence.

The nasty, disgusting curse words,
I make them sit back by the wall.
Seldom used, they have a bad attitude,
and would rather go smoke in the hall.

Some anxious words try to jump in
and disrupt the conversation.
Rational words have to set them all straight,
to resume cooperation.

Words with more than one meaning,
and nouns arrive late every time.
We're anxious to hear their adventures,
in someone else's rhyme.

Some words don't want to be here;
my poems have not passed their test.
I'm not controversial enough;
their absence is all for the best.

As I sat at the desk then writing,
there appeared a distinguished word,
who calmly sauntered into the space.
It was vintage and now seldom heard.

That group was composed in the shadows,
with a wise and deliberate air.
Fully aware I would realize,
there were no other words to compare.

With so many words to choose from,
I hired the group of word leaders
to organize and collect my thoughts,
to be new idea greeters.

Well, the power of words corrupted them,
using lies to deceive and degrade,
pitting one group against another.
I fired them…and made them behave.

Now all the words come to me freely;
each group has something to say.
I give them a subject, and they discuss,
with each sentence, their roles on display.

To collaborate with them, exciting!
Fine ideas poured out on the page.
The thrill escapes all definition.
Our mission: a message conveyed.

Words express the human condition,
with passions, hopes, fears we entrust.
Words give us a sense of control,
but be mindful…they don't control us!

November 18, 2021

Perception

There's an old pane of glass in my window
with charming ripples and waves that flow,
the results of a skill practiced long ago.

I peer out on the world and realize
I can see the glass, like a veil or disguise,
slightly distorting the view on my side.

As if the glass has something to say,
it reveals the scenery in its own way,
and challenges me in visual play.

We go back and forth but neither one wins,
which only makes me smile and grin,
because looking out, makes me look within.

Like the once molten pane of my old window,
our minds have ripples and waves, and so,
we perceive the world through what we know.

Our perceptions are but a flow of thought,
a melding of sorts, of all that is wrought,
rendering argument all for naught.

Understanding the structure brings clarity.
We must adjust our position to see
a new view through another reality.

February 18, 2012

Sides

We are right and they are wrong;
the truth is how we see that.
Our courage and conviction strong,
lifetimes engaged in combat.

It matters not how many die,
as long as it's not us.
We have valid reasons why
it's they who cause mistrust.

Our children know our bloody plight,
for our souls we pray,
for courage through explosive nights,
and vengeance to repay.

Their children the unworthy ones,
our hatred they compel.
Inhuman are their evil sons,
damn them all to hell.

Our holy land is so profound;
significance they lack.
We'll wage war on hallowed ground,
now bound to take it back.

Our truth and our religion are
the reasons they must fall.
We're holier than they by far,
as proof…we'll kill them all.

The Beltline

My vehicle,
mechanical motion
at stationary speeds.

Each separate, in this same place.
A kinetic symbiosis
of different minds.

Limited pathways
inching closer,
determined by circumstance.

Adeptly guided, left then right,
leading then following,
maintaining distance.

Reactions born of instinct,
choices in the moment,
impact on the outcome.

Time bringing closure
to the journey's destination,
a return to the beginning.

Winter 2001

Message of My Journals

All the words know what they mean,
to read, confront the truth.
I've written them in hopes that you
will need no further proof.

I dwelled upon the earth as this
and drew on every source,
intuitively reasoning,
embarked on every course.

A body here conforming to
a place, a time, event,
precariously balancing,
perception, truth, intent.

Ever questioning the answers,
daily droning numbs my mind.
Useless information veils
authentic life design.

My very thoughts now hindering
my quest, I seek a goal
to release my burdened ignorance,
my consciousness console.

Therein lies the clarity,
a knowing freed by will.
The truth is there, has always been,
through soul, life is fulfilled.

In each of us God animates
reality sublime.
Creation manifests in us,
unified, divine.

May 20, 2005

Hostage

Here it is again,
though I do not recognize it for what it is.
I am intoxicated with it;
I can smell my own skin!

The sweet perfumes of life swirl about me with each breath.
This intensely heightened sense of smell distracts
me from the truth.
I am ignorant of its warning.

Were it numbing lips or geometric lights seen behind my
closed eyes, I would have known at once.
Too much time has gone by now, and I am again besieged.
My body becomes nauseated.

Tightness in my throat signals that chemicals from
the pill I have taken are now in my system,
but it is too late; they do nothing to release me.

I am a hostage.
My captor shows no compassion;
it knows none.
Unrelenting force of pressure grips and binds me to the pain.

There is no weapon, though the pain
inflicted is profound and relentless.
Tears leak uncontrollably at the corners of my eyes.
There is no defense.
Even surrender is not freeing.

I can only endure through the torturous pain.

Would that I had some dark secret or coveted knowledge
to reveal that would end the torment, I would speak it now,
but there are no such demands,
no negotiation for my release.

If time is a constant, how does it pass so slowly now?
That part of my brain which is reptilian
solely accounts for my existence in these hours.

Only the passage of time can change my circumstance,
only that which passes, unaware of me,
and I count on it.

At last I emerge unceremoniously,
weak, exhausted, and free for now to resume my life,
less that which was taken.

I rationalize that others have survived far worse fates than mine,
far worse than the misery I suffer in the prison of my assailant,
far worse than the unwitting cruelty inflicted
in the throes of a migraine.

January 13, 2008

There

In a place where color and darkness fuse,
every breath draws in light.

Where the cosmic dust of all the things that once mattered,
float by unattended and unlamented.

Subconscious rhythmic force drowns it out,
brain numbing diffusion, confusion
— noise.

It's all so clear, beyond reality,
past all that appears to be so.

It's not.

It's like a great, ferocious guard dog,
that keeps us from knowing
the true power of things as they are.

September 26, 2007

The Design

Each life is a vivid creation,
shaped by a perfect design,
unique on its own,
but truth to be shown,
its existence is duly entwined.

Every life influenced by others,
all sides of our nature, a part.
All of us needed,
the puzzle completed,
a living mosaic of art!

November 25, 2011

Good Idea

I had a good idea,
I thought the whole thing through,
worked out every detail,
each element reviewed.

Impassioned in the moment
my creative process thrived.
Time and space conforming,
in my mind, it was derived.

How simple in its structure,
it made such perfect sense.
Surely others thought of this,
though lacking evidence.

Pure genius! I conferred
with myself, truly profound…
though now I can't remember it
…I didn't write it down!

2013

Dead Piano

As I drove around the corner
to my horror there it lay,
turned over on its chest,
a most terrible display.

How did it come to be there?
Did it put up any fight?
What violence had taken place
that led now to this sight?

Through the door and down the stairs,
in pieces on the walk.
What happened to you, you poor thing?
If only you could talk!

What thoughtless act of mayhem,
what compelled the person there,
to think there was no life left
in the music…such despair!

I thought that I should call someone,
report this dreadful crime,
"Police, come quick, a murder
of the most abhorrent kind."

I cannot take my eyes off it.
I cannot drive my car.
Shock has taken over,
and I don't know where we are.

"Let's go," the person next to me
is saying in my ear,
but I'm frozen in the moment
and just don't seem to hear.

My heart is reaching out
as I comprehend the toll.
The death of a piano
resonates deep in my soul.

June 18, 2003

Empty Boxes

In our big house there are many rooms,
each function explicitly set.
The interesting ones are storing our things
whose values aren't obvious yet.

Lingering memories from times now past,
children's schoolwork, drawings, and notes,
pictures and papers and cards of all sorts,
well preserved in boxes and totes.

Receipts so old that the ink disappeared,
some so old, they are no longer needed.
Others were kept to remember the "deal,"
such a sale that could not be repeated!

There's a large box of gifts for the kids,
not given out yet for some reason.
One or two, too many for birthdays,
or bought in the holiday season.

Decorative items moved here, from there,
undecided have nowhere to go.
Their value in question, just waiting for me.
Rummage sale...keep? I don't know!

I'll save all the schoolwork and kids' stuff,
look through cards; there's still money in some!
Hey this is important! How'd it get here?
I'll file till my fingers are numb.

There's a box-full that's only important to me;
when I'm gone it will be thrown away.
They'll wonder why I had saved all that stuff,
and I won't be there to say.

After reading and sorting and filing,
crying and laughing out loud,
all of our memories of moments
are at home with the file cabinet crowd.

Still there in the corner fixed neatly,
a straight tower stacked larger to small,
an assemblage of marvelous boxes
with nothing inside them at all.

Nothing but still smaller boxes,
inside, smaller yet as they go,
nesting inside of each other.
How many are there? I don't know.

They're durable, fine, and clean,
and vary in shape and color.
Holding only boxes right now,
they'll be used, for some reason or other.

I have questioned myself why I keep them.
Surely more are made every day,
but these are *very nice* boxes,
and I just can't throw them away!

Someday they'll hold something special,
a gift to someone I love.
A specific size will be needed,
and I'll *have* one that fits like a glove!

Dad used to bring home boxes;
we played with them hours on end!
Making up uses and stories,
getting lost in the land of pretend.

I *will* find a use for those boxes,
yes, it seems that I always do.
They're a tower of hope for the future
and perhaps hold a memory or two!

April 25, 2020

Being

Do you feel what I am thinking
as you go forth through your day?
Do you know what I am feeling
as you file your thoughts away?

I sense you all around me
though there's miles between us two,
a connection of such substance
not defined by known value.

Within I have the notion
that I'm never quite alone,
thoughts to me unique,
not exclusively my own.

When I look down, I see hands
I don't recognize as mine.
I ponder who I am or was
and how I am defined.

A separate life connected
to a universal whole,
who share the thoughts of all
that have known its earthy toll.

Sometimes I can feel your thoughts,
your feelings known to me,
or the ache of pending doom,
forewarns of tragedy.

There's no question I am not alone,
this body's not just "me",
but a conduit of consciousness,
eternal energy.

August 20, 2003

Life

Rolling from the depths,
waves in rhythmic bands,
washing onto shore,
to soothe the shifting sands.

As calming as a friend,
a voice that speaks with reason,
the sea knows only truth,
as witness to all seasons.

Love made whole then gone,
as fickle as the moon.
Emotions high and low,
with the tide we are in tune.

But even as the winds may change
and ships choose not to land,
constant are the waves
that soothe the shifting sands.

A broken shell or bottle,
like dreams and plans and fears,
adrift upon the waters,
cast there throughout the years.

Now are treasured gems,
rubbed smooth by pounding rifts,
then deposited on shore,
like sentimental gifts.

Tragedy upon us,
winter storms atop the sea,
frozen in our state,
distressed humanity.

But beneath the winter ice,
patient waters understand,
waiting for the chance,
to soothe the shifting sands.

The shoreline reaching out,
swept away by undertow,
in the depths encounter that
which above you would not know.

A world of teeming life
only glimpsed if from a distance.
There inside the soul,
new dimensions of existence.

Lives transformed by change
in a grand or subtle stage,
are soothed by rolling waves
of acceptance, washed with age.

Time's renewing waters,
which temper life's demands,
show compassion for our choices,
soothe our lives…the shifting sands.

March 20, 2009

Acknowledgements

My poems are a product of my outlook and perspective and are admittedly skewed, as a product of all that has influenced my life. I would like to acknowledge the people who have affected and inspired me along the way.

My parents, Don and Adele, (who have already passed) have both inspired me. Adele, who was truly creative, made everything she did a perfect work of art. Though my mother was an accomplished artist, she never had the means to finish her studies at the Art Institute of Chicago, opting to buy food instead, after suffering from a bout of malnutrition. She never lamented this to her children, and I only know of it through one specific conversation when I asked about her past. She lived for her husband and five children, and prayed to God to keep her alive and well until all of us were grown. While discussing daily life as a mom, she had confessed that there were months and yes, years that she did not remember anything in particular that happened. With that realization, she became my inspiration to start writing things down.

Don always hoped to pen a great story, and in the scant amount of time outside his work-a-day world as a meatcutter, he took in books and articles of various genres, aspiring to be a writer himself. He critiqued movies and shows as we watched them, pointing out flaws, interjecting how it should have been written noting, *you should always write about a subject you know, and each role must always remain true to their character for the story to ring true.* He was particularly critical of war movies, knowing firsthand what really happened in World War II. At a particularly intense scene, heightened by the crescendo of an orchestra, I remember he leaned over to look me in the eye as he commented, "There was no music in the war." His passion for writing and the significance he attached to it, also inspired me to write.

I thank my parents for their sacrifices and inspiration. Sadly, Don and Adele never had the chance to read any of my poems.

My siblings, Donna, David, Adele and Theresa, though not directly involved in my writing, have shared their lives with me, and in turn contributed to my memories and helped shape my perspective and influenced my outlook on life. Our connections have meant the world to me and I thank them for their impact on my life.

My husband, Peter, has been mentioned in the poems by name many times, which appropriately reflects our 40 years of marriage. Of those, the last 20 years he has been reading and commenting on my poems. I check in with him on details, as we have spent many eventful years of life together, all just waiting to become poems.

My two daughters, Amanda and Nicole, have contributed through our unique connection and conversations. They take me back to things they remember, and their perspectives and insights have been invaluable to my understanding of the world as I know it. At times our banter has led us to uncontrollable laughter, as we find ourselves the most humorous of all subjects. I thank them for their support and encouragement to send these poems out into the world.

I want to thank Shelley B. who has encouraged me to write every time we see each other. The poem that she wrote in our Brother Dutton School was such an inspiring work of art, that I felt the need in turn, to write a note of creative poetic acknowledgement to her. Thank you, Shelley, for your encouragement, it has meant a great deal more than you know.

Thank you to Orange Hat Publishing and Ten16 Press for publishing my book of poetry and taking a chance on me. Thank you to their staff for walking me through the process with patience, affirmation and support. Working with them has truly been a pleasure.

CPSIA information can be obtained
at www.ICGtesting.com
Printed in the USA
JSHW022317011222
34198JS00002B/3